W9-BDV-596

MESSENGER PUBLIC LIBRARY
NORTH AURORA, ILLINOIS

EDGE
BOOKS™

THIS or THAT

ANIMAL

Debate

A RiP-ROARiNG GAME OF EiTHER/OR QUESTiONS

BY JOAN AXELROD-CONTRADA

CAPSTONE PRESS
a capstone imprint

Edge Books are published by Capstone Press,
1710 Roe Crest Drive, North Mankato, Minnesota 56003.
www.capstonepub.com

Copyright © 2013 by Capstone Press, a Capstone imprint.
All rights reserved.
No part of this publication may be reproduced in whole or in part,
or stored in a retrieval system, or transmitted in any form or by any means,
electronic, mechanical, photocopying, recording, or otherwise, without
written permission of the publisher.
For information regarding permission, write to Capstone Press,
1710 Roe Crest Drive, North Mankato, Minnesota 56003.

Library of Congress Cataloging-in-Publication Data
Axelrod-Contrada, Joan.
  This or that animal debate : a rip-roaring game of either/or questions / by Joan
    Axelrod-Contrada.
    p. cm. — (Edge books. This or that?)
  Summary: "Offers intriguing either/or questions and content on animal topics to
    encourage critical thinking and debate"—Provided by publisher.
  ISBN 978-1-4296-8593-1 (library binding)
  ISBN 978-1-4296-9272-4 (paperback)
  ISBN 978-1-62065-237-4 (ebook PDF)
  1. Animals—Miscellanea—Juvenile literature. I. Title.
  QL49.A893 2013
  590—dc23
                                    2012006494

Editorial Credits

Kristen Mohn, editor; Veronica Correia, designer; Eric Gohl, media researcher;
    Laura Manthe, production specialist

Photo Credits

AP Images: LM Otero, 19, Middletown Journal/Pat Auckerman, 8; Corbis: Ecoscene/
Frank Blackburn, 29; Dreamstime: Asther Lau Choon Siew, 27, Jagronick, 10;
iStockphotos: Eric Delmar, 22, Jim Kruger, 13; Minden Pictures: Mark Moffett, 28;
Newscom: EPA/Nic Bothma, 11, Photoshot/Evolve/Stephen Dalton, 21, Zuma Press,
5; Shutterstock: abeadev, cover, AISPIX by Image Source, 16, Binkski, backgrounds,
Chad Littlejohn, 3, 25, Dave Pusey, 14, Fedor Selivanov, 1, 20, FotoVeto, 6, Jason
Prince, 15, JSseng, 24, Karen Hadley, 17, Mircea Bezergheanu, 23, pat138241,
9, photobar, 12, Ronald van der Beek, 4, Simon Greig, 26, Stas Volik, 18, Vadim
Petrakov, 7

Printed in the United States of America in Stevens Point, Wisconsin.
032012   006678WZF12

How to Use This Book:

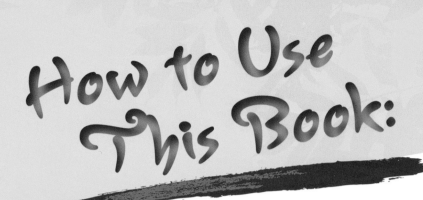

Have you ever wished you could climb walls like a gecko or walk on water like a basilisk lizard? What if you had to pick one or the other?

This book is full of questions that take you inside the weird and wacky world of animals—their behavior, their defenses, and all their amazing abilities. Each question is followed by information to help you weigh the options and come to a decision. But don't worry—it's not a test! There are no right or wrong answers.

When you are finished reading the book, try it out on your family and friends. Debate them on the pros and cons of wrestling a bear or swimming with a shark … which would they choose?

THIS

A PET CHIMPANZEE

- seven times stronger than humans
- banned as pets in 21 states
- 98 percent genetically the same as humans

Pet chimps can learn to paint, play soccer, dress themselves, and play drums. Some have even learned sign language. They're playful as babies. Many, though, turn aggressive as adults. They can also be unpredictable. In one case, a male chimp attacked his owner's friend and bit off her face. The chimp knew the friend, but possibly didn't recognize her because she was wearing a new hairstyle.

OR THAT?

A PET PYTHON

- can grow to more than 20 feet (6 meters) long
- can weigh 200 pounds (91 kilograms)
- may frighten your friends

Cold-blooded. Dangerous. Pythons are not your typical pet. They wrap themselves around their prey to strangle them. They sometimes swallow their victims whole. Pythons killed 12 humans between 1980 and 2009. However, pythons kill fewer people a year than dogs do. Dogs fatally attacked 88 people in a recent three-year period. Pythons can be safe pets as long as they are kept enclosed in proper cages.

THIS

TO TRAIN A CROW

- crows mimic sounds
- able to play tricks on one another
- make and use tools

Bird brains? Hardly. Crows are highly intelligent. They can make sounds like cats, dogs, and geese, and they can mimic human speech. They can make tools, such as hooks to reach food. Crows can also recognize people's faces. The U.S. military even thought of using crows to locate terrorist Osama bin Laden. Crows hold grudges against people who annoy them. When angry, they'll swoop down and attack with their claws and beaks. Those claws and beaks can also be helpful. Scientists are hoping to train crows to pick up garbage.

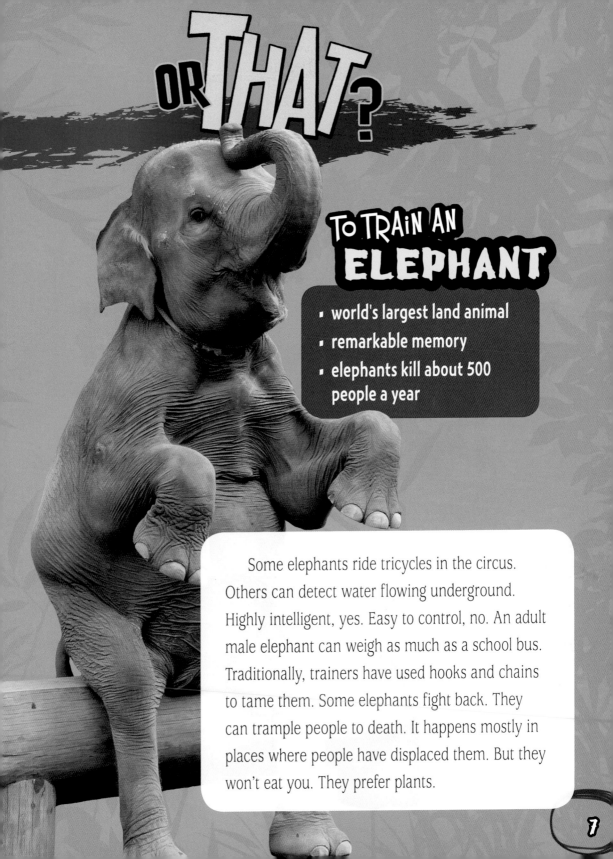

OR THAT?

TO TRAIN AN ELEPHANT

- world's largest land animal
- remarkable memory
- elephants kill about 500 people a year

Some elephants ride tricycles in the circus. Others can detect water flowing underground. Highly intelligent, yes. Easy to control, no. An adult male elephant can weigh as much as a school bus. Traditionally, trainers have used hooks and chains to tame them. Some elephants fight back. They can trample people to death. It happens mostly in places where people have displaced them. But they won't eat you. They prefer plants.

THIS

TO WRESTLE A BLACK BEAR

- male bears weigh up to 600 pounds (272 kg)
- killed more than 60 people in 100 years
- mostly vegetarian

In the wild, male bears wrestle one another when battling for a female's attention. When humans wrestle bears, it's usually to entertain a crowd. It dates back to the carnivals and county fairs of the 1800s, but it's now outlawed in many states. The goal is to bring the bear to the ground, pinning its backside to the floor. But the huge animals outweigh humans by hundreds of pounds. No wonder people call bear wrestling an extreme sport.

OR THAT?

TO WRESTLE AN ALLIGATOR

- alligators killed 17 people in 60 years
- weigh 450 to 600 pounds (204 to 272 kg); up to 18 feet (5.5 m) long
- brain smaller than a tablespoon

Snap! An alligator crushes its prey. Occasionally the victim is a person. Alligators, though, prefer smaller prey. More people eat alligators than the other way around. Some people in Florida wrestle alligators for sport. The wrestlers hold the gators down and try to squeeze their jaws shut. Or they hold the jaws open and put their heads inside the gators' mouths. Some people say alligator wrestling is cruel to the animals. Others insist that the only danger is to the humans.

THIS

GREAT WHITE SHARK

- largest predatory fish on Earth
- 300 teeth—serrated like steak knives
- 79 attacks on humans worldwide in 2010

Great white sharks weigh as much as full-sized pickup trucks. They feed on seals, sea lions, dolphins, small whales, and fish, including other sharks. Usually, they limit their taste of humans to a single bite. If the bite is large, the victim can die. Some researchers think great whites mistake humans for their regular food. Other experts believe the sharks bite out of curiosity. Between 2000 and 2010, only 7 percent of shark attacks were fatal. Sharks are particularly attracted to bright colors. Researchers jokingly refer to yellow as the "yum yum" color.

OR THAT?

TO SWiM WiTH A BOX JELLYFISH

- have among the deadliest venom in the animal kingdom
- kill 100 people a year
- can cause death within minutes

Box jellyfish combine beauty with danger. Long tentacles trail from their amazing see-through bodies. Their tiny stinging cells shoot deadly venom. Box jellyfish live in tropical waters near Australia, Vietnam, Hawaii, and the Philippines. Since the first reported death more than 100 years ago, 68 percent of people stung by box jellyfish have died. Fortunately, fewer people are dying from box jellyfish these days. Many beaches have installed "stinger nets" to keep jellyfish out of swimming zones. Treating stings with vinegar and wearing special protective clothing helps too.

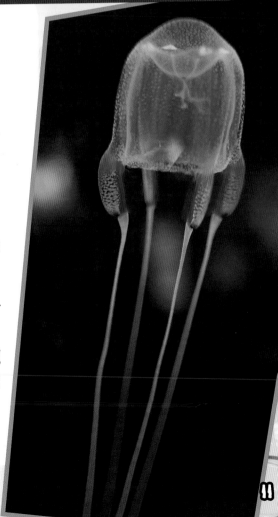

THIS

TO SPRINT LIKE A
CHEETAH

- world's fastest land animal; can run up to 70 miles (113 kilometers) per hour
- catches prey 7 out of every 10 chases
- long recovery time after running

Cheetahs can outrun cars on the highway. They need their speed to catch gazelles and other quick-moving animals. They can sprint at top speed only for 20 to 60 seconds before they overheat and need to rest. It takes 20 minutes for their breathing and body temperature to return to normal. They're too tired during this recovery period to defend their food. They lose it to other animals half of the time.

OR THAT?

TO RUN LONG DISTANCES LIKE A WOLF

- high stamina
- can run 22 miles (35 km) without stopping
- top speed of 40 miles (64 km) per hour

Wolves are built for traveling long distances. They must roam far and wide to find their meals. They hunt in packs to attack herds of deer, moose, and other large animals. Many of the quick sprinters get away. But wolves use their stamina to wear down the weakest members of the herd. One wolf might devour 20 pounds (9 kg) in a single meal. That's like eating 80 hamburgers in one sitting. After that, they can go for several days without eating.

THIS

TO BE CHASED BY A
HIPPOPOTAMUS

- hippos kill more than 200 people a year
- weigh 5,000 to 8,000 pounds (2,268 to 3,629 kg)
- run as fast as humans for short distances

Hippos eat plants, not people. Still, they're among the most dangerous and aggressive of all animals in Africa. Less solitary than rhinos, hippos generally live in groups of 10 to 30 animals. When in water, hippos have been known to chase boatloads of people. Hippos bare their large teeth when feeling threatened. They can run up to 14 miles (22.5 km) per hour on land. Humans killed by hippos are usually trampled or crushed to death.

OR THAT?

TO BE CHASED BY A
RHINOCEROS

- rhinos are dangerous when startled
- may weigh up to 7,000 pounds (3,175 kg)
- can run 40 miles (64 km) per hour

Rhino size varies by species, with some even larger than hippos. They're built like tanks, with plated skin as armor. Found in both Asia and Africa, rhinos eat plants. They like to wallow in the mud to keep cool. Lazy? Not always. If they smell an unfamiliar scent, they'll get nervous. That's why they attack humans. They're not trying to eat you—they're just defending themselves. Their sharp horns can grow up to 5 feet (1.5 m) long, and they use them to stab enemies.

THIS

TO BE RAISED BY WILD DOGS

- skilled hunters
- feed vomit to their young
- extremely loyal to their pack

Dogs are loyal pack animals. Wild dogs will search for days for a missing pack member. Thanks to good teamwork, 70 to 90 percent of their hunts end in a kill, compared to only 30 to 40 percent for lions. A few human children have lived with wild dogs. News reports tell the story of Oxana Malaya. A neglected child, she moved into a shack with a pack of wild dogs at age 3. Five years later, people tried to rescue her. The dogs wouldn't let them near her at first. Oxana behaved like a dog, eating scraps of raw meat and moving on all fours.

OR THAT?

TO BE RAISED BY
MONKEYS

- most species are 93 percent genetically the same as humans
- communicate using variety of sounds
- sleep in trees

Vervet monkeys live in close family groups. They groom one another and even help babysit their younger siblings. Several years ago, a boy named John Ssebunya lived among vervet monkeys in Uganda. He escaped into the forest at the age of 2 or 3 after a family tragedy. The monkeys brought him food. He lived on fruit, nuts, and berries and learned to raid nearby banana fields. When villagers tried to rescue John, he hurled sticks at them. His monkey friends tried to protect him. After his rescue, John learned to speak and even joined a children's choir.

THIS

TO SPEW VOMIT LIKE A
TURKEY VULTURE

- eats dead flesh
- can detect carcass scent from 200 feet (61 m) in the air
- vomits when startled

Turkey vultures vomit as a defense. These big birds like to eat in peace. When another animal interrupts its meal, the turkey vulture throws up some of its freshly eaten food. A vulture eats big meals, so vomiting helps relieve it of extra weight. Then it's light enough to fly again and make a quick get-away. In addition, vomiting gives other animals a free meal. Would-be predators gobble up the vomit instead of the turkey vulture.

OR THAT?

TO SQUIRT BLOOD FROM YOUR EYES LIKE A REGAL HORNED LIZARD

- able to squirt blood from eyes up to 5 feet (1.5 m)
- large spiky crown
- slower than other lizards

Regal horned lizards give new meaning to the phrase "blood-shot eyes." When threatened, they squirt blood from the corners of their eyes. They do this by bursting tiny blood vessels. The spray of fresh blood startles and repulses their enemies. A horned lizard uses other defenses first. It tries to hide. It puffs up its body to look scarier. But if enemies won't back down, the lizard increases the blood pressure in its head. Then it shoots out a powerful stream of blood. Usually the other animal flees the scene.

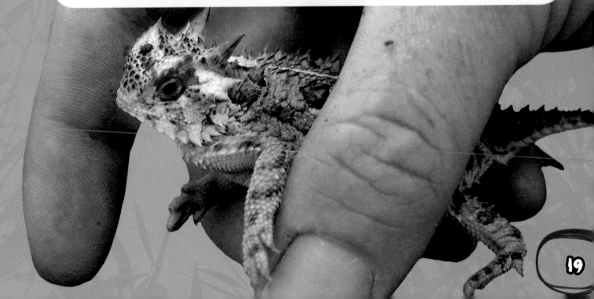

THIS

TO CLIMB WALLS LIKE A GECKO

- climbs trees
- can walk upside down
- inspired human inventors

Geckos have superpowers. The Tokay gecko from Asia can scamper along walls and ceilings, thanks to the millions of tiny sticky hairs on the pads of its feet. This colorful, chirping lizard is one of the largest in the lizard family. Scientists inspired by this gecko have created a new kind of tape. Tiny plastic fibers act like the hairs on the gecko's feet. Other products, such as special gloves for mountain climbers, might follow.

OR THAT?

TO WALK ON WATER LiKE A BASILISK LIZARD

- weighs about 7 ounces (0.2 kg)
- runs across water at speeds of 5 to 7 miles (8 to 11 km) per hour
- takes 20 steps per second

Basilisk lizards do the seemingly impossible—they walk on water. Actually, they run on water. They create air pockets when they slap the water. This helps keep them from sinking or tipping over. They use their special skill to get away from enemies. Humans can only imagine walking on water. Some engineers, though, have created a robot that can do just that.

THIS

TO EAT LIKE A PIG

- can weigh up to 1,000 pounds (454 kg)
- digs for root foods
- heavy hogs earn more money for farmers

What does it mean to eat like a pig? Pigs eat just about anything. Although mostly vegetarian, they'll eat dead insects, worms, and even dead pigs if given the chance. According to some experts, though, pigs don't overeat—they just eat until they are full. Others insist that they do, in fact, "pig out." How so? They eat with their mouths open. They smack their lips. They eat quickly. And they eat a lot. A piglet weighs about 2.5 pounds (1 kg) at birth. By the time it's 6 months old, it can weigh up to 220 pounds (100 kg).

OR THAT?

TO EAT LIKE A BIRD

- needs a lot of food for flying
- feasts before migrating
- some birds eat chunks of flesh

Someone who "eats like a bird" hardly eats anything at all. Birds, though, eat a lot for their size. Most birds fly, which takes a lot of energy. They get their energy from food. Some eat more than half their weight in food each day. How much a bird eats varies by species and season. Hummingbirds might eat every four or five minutes to get the sugar they need. Migrating birds will eat almost their full weight in food to fuel up for a long trip. Birds of prey use their sharp bills to tear the flesh they eat. How's that for eating like a bird?

THIS

TO BE A QUEEN BEE

- rules over thousands
- bigger than other bees
- lays 200,000 eggs a year

QUEEN BEE

The queen bee is basically an "egg-laying machine." After mating, the queen lays eggs nonstop for the next two or three years. She produces them at a frantic pace of one egg a minute. If she fails to lay enough eggs, the worker bees can turn on her. They'll feed "royal jelly" to a special group of bees. These queens-in-waiting will fight one another to death until only one remains. The workers then kill off the old queen. But some lucky queens rule for life.

OR THAT?

TO BE A LION KING

- lives in groups of about 15
- may share power with other males
- kills off cubs not his own

Male lions are sometimes called "lazy." After all, they let females do most of the hunting. Still, they earn their keep by defending and protecting their group against intruders. A lion's social group, or "pride," consists mostly of females and their young. Young males are kicked out of the pride when they are 2 to 3 years old. The outcast males roam the wild. Some live on their own forever. Others join a new pride by battling the existing males for control. The fights can be deadly. However, males that surrender by lying on their backs may be allowed to leave in peace. Usually there's no one clear "lion king." Instead, a few males rule together as a group.

THIS

TO LIVE IN A SKYSCRAPER LIKE A TERMITE

- termite mounds can be as high as 30 feet (9 m)
- millions of termites live together
- chimneys release gas and heat

Termite mounds have all the comforts of home. Heating. Air conditioning. Even nurseries for the young. The tiny insects make their homes out of their waste, saliva, and soil. The mounds can take centuries to build. Termites dislike being too hot or too cold. The skyscrapers keep them warm in the morning and cool later in the day. The termites eat fungi and also chomp on dead wood, which they keep in special cubbies. The eye-catching mounds can be found in Australia, Africa, and Central and South America. Abandoned mounds serve other animals. Squirrels might move in. Cheetahs and leopards sometimes use the mounds as lookout towers.

OR THAT?

TO LiVE iN A MOBiLE HOME LiKE A DECORATOR CRAB

- attaches other creatures to its shell
- master of disguise
- recycles its decorations

Decorator crabs carry their homes on their backs. They dress up their shells with bits of seaweed, sponges, and anemones. Some species use Velcrolike hooks to stick on the decorations. Others produce a sticky substance from their mouths. The plant and animal coverings help them blend in with the sea floor. In addition, some decorations protect them from their enemies. Fish find some sponges bad tasting or poisonous. When decorator crabs outgrow their shells, they grow new ones. But they're not wasteful. They attach their old decorations to the new shell.

THIS

TO BE A
JUMPING SPIDER
PRETENDING TO BE AN ANT

- spider looks and acts like an ant
- lives with ants
- teams up with ants to fight predators

JUMPING SPIDER

Why would a spider want to be an ant? Easy—ants don't taste good! Many predators avoid ants because they taste like acid. The jumping spider has adapted to look and act like an ant to fool its predators. It even raises its two front legs to look like ant antennae. The ants accept the spider as one of their own. The spider also benefits by being part of a large, powerful ant colony. Together they gang up on prey. Then the spider helps itself to its share of the meal—which often includes other spiders.

TO BE A
CUCKOO BIRD
IN ANOTHER BIRD'S NEST

- kicks other chicks out of the nest
- larger than other chicks
- gets free food

Cuckoos are masters of trickery. Many species lay their eggs in the nests of other birds. The cuckoo mother chooses only the nests of other insect-eating songbirds. The cuckoo chick hatches before the songbird's eggs. It then kicks the other chicks out of the nest. The cuckoo is able to mimic the cries of its new family. It can even sound like many chicks at once so the mother will bring more food! The mother feeds it as if it were her own. The cuckoo gets the food and nest to itself.

SONGBIRD MOTHER

CUCKOO CHICK

Lightning Round:

▶ Would you choose to be able to LIFT HEAVY OBJECTS LIKE A GORILLA or DIVE AS DEEP AS A SPERM WHALE?

▶ Would you choose to live inside a HUMAN'S INTESTINES LIKE A TAPEWORM or SUCK HUMAN BLOOD LIKE A LEECH?

▶ Would you choose to defend yourself with a SKUNK'S STINKY SPRAY or a PORCUPINE'S SHARP QUILLS?

▶ Would you choose to develop in a COCOON LIKE A BUTTERFLY or in a POUCH LIKE A KANGAROO?

▶ Would you choose to grab your prey with a RATTLESNAKE'S FANGS or a BALD EAGLE'S CLAWS?

▶ Would you choose to SLEEP UPSIDE DOWN LIKE A BAT or ON ONE LEG LIKE A FLAMINGO?

▶ Would you choose to be EATEN BY YOUR MOTHER LIKE A SCORPION or BY YOUR MATE LIKE A PRAYING MANTIS?

▶ Would you choose to show your anger by SPITTING LIKE A LLAMA or TURNING DIFFERENT COLORS LIKE A CHAMELEON?

▶ Would you choose to have a nose like A STAR-NOSED MOLE or A PROBOSCIS MONKEY?

▶ Would you choose to drink a PERSON'S SWEAT LIKE A BUTTERFLY or LAY YOUR EGGS IN MAMMAL POOP LIKE A DUNG BEETLE?

- Would you choose to be able to PULL YOUR HEAD IN YOUR SHELL LIKE A TURTLE or HIDE IN PLAIN SIGHT LIKE A WALKING STICK?

- Would you choose to be able to DIVE 200 MILES (322 KM) PER HOUR LIKE A PEREGRINE FALCON or BE HEARD 3 MILES (4.8 KM) AWAY LIKE A HOWLER MONKEY?

- Would you choose to EAT YOUR OWN POOP LIKE A RABBIT or SOMEONE ELSE'S DROPPINGS LIKE A COTTONSTAINER BUG?

- Would you choose to have your mate FEED YOU BREAKFAST IN BED LIKE A CARDINAL or BUILD YOU A NEST LIKE A BOWERBIRD?

- Would you choose to find your way by USING THE SUN LIKE A BEE or THE STARS LIKE A BIRD TRAVELING AT NIGHT?

- Would you choose to fool predators with FAKE EYES LIKE A FOUREYE BUTTERFLY FISH or a FAKE HEAD LIKE SOME CATERPILLARS?

- Would you choose to HEAR SOUNDS MILES AWAY LIKE AN ELEPHANT or SEE A MILLION DIFFERENT COLORS LIKE A MANTIS SHRIMP?

- Would you choose to BATHE WITH YOUR TONGUE LIKE A CAT or IN THE DIRT LIKE A SPARROW?

Read More

Allen, Kathy. *Elephants Under Pressure: A Cause and Effect Investigation.* Animals on the Edge. Mankato, Minn.: Capstone Press, 2011.

Bloom, Steve. *My Favorite Animal Families.* New York: Thames & Hudson, 2010.

McPhee, Margaret. *Weird and Wonderful: Show-offs.* Astonishing Animals, Bizarre Behavior. New York: Kingfisher, 2011.

Phillips, Adam. *Amazing Animals.* Hauppauge, N.Y.: Barrons Educational Series, Inc., 2011.

Internet Sites

FactHound offers a safe, fun way to find Internet sites related to this book. All of the sites on FactHound have been researched by our staff.

Here's all you do:

Visit *www.facthound.com*

Type in this code: 9781429685931

Super-cool stuff! Check out projects, games and lots more at
www.capstonekids.com